Discover Your Identity

A guide to discovering your personal identity

Jennifer Lynn Adams

a Flying Chickadee publication

Discover Your Identity
A guide to discovering your personal identity
By Jennifer Lynn Adams

ISBN-13: 978-0-9896263-4-7
ISBN-10: 0989626342

First printing, March 2015
Flying Chickadee
PO Box 30021, Seattle, WA 98113-0021
www.flyingchickadee.com

Photograph on front cover by Laurie Lynn
Photograph on back cover by Sarah Sage
Book editing, design and layout by Flying Chickadee

CONTENTS

INTRODUCTION: DISCOVER YOUR IDENTITY

"There is no greater joy in life than knowing who you are and feeling confident in your identity!"

Life is a series of seasons and in each season you learn new things about yourself. Knowing who you are is a journey, a journey worth taking. Sometimes the journey is arduous and you may feel like giving up, but if you press through the difficult times, you will shine on the other side. As you walk the path of discovering your identity, you will mature and grow along the way.

Most of my life, I have struggled with fear and anxiety. At times it has plagued me to the point of being hospitalized. Not the psych ward, but the ER, due to severe anemia, infection and abnormally fast heartbeat. There were seasons in my life during which I couldn't see or fathom who I was because I was in survival mode. But thank God I had people in my life that led me to the deep, refreshing waters of truth, and there I found myself. I have overcome fear and it no longer rules my existence or experience of life. Now I have the privilege of living life adventurously, fully aware of my identity, my destiny and my purpose.

Finding yourself is like reuniting with an old friend that you lost somewhere along the way. There is no greater joy in life than knowing who you are and feeling confident in your identity! We cannot deny that we live in trying times, just turn on the news and we see it. The world desperately needs citizens who know who they are. The world needs people who are living for a purpose. When you know who you are you will become a force of positive change in the world. When you know who you are, you will become empowered to influence the world around you.

This book delves into the sub-topics of personal identity. There are reflective questions and action steps at the end of every chapter to inspire you to dig deep into who you are. The first step in the journey to discovering your identity is to have the desire to know who you are and be a student of yourself. My intention in writing this book is that it will provide guidance in your journey towards discovering your identity.

CHAPTER 1:
MY STORY

"The experience of belonging healed the hurt of my past and the dark clouds of doubt and fear began to dissipate. I could see a good future ahead of me."

My life journey has been one of miracles that have gotten me to today, one miracle after another and many more on the horizon. I was born with partial limbs. Due to a lack of resources and personal issues my biological parents were not able to care for me. I was adopted by my parents at birth, the first miracle of my life. I was raised in a big family – six of us were adopted and have special needs, and my parents also had two children biologically. I am most grateful to my parents for advocating for my independence and education. One of the things they did best was to nurture my gregarious personality, and my gifts and talents of singing and public speaking. I started voice lessons when I was six years old with my vocal coach Melody. She was a very influential person in my upbringing and became like an Auntie to me. Her influence was especially important during my difficult adolescent years.

My early childhood was really good. I lived in a great neighborhood, with lots of other kids. It was middle school when the issues of bullying began to be introduced in my life. School became a warzone of hurtful words, threats to my well-being and peer rejection. I was scared to go to school. The bullying continued through high school and my self-esteem diminished. I became anorexic in high school, trying to find a way to be accepted. It was my voice teacher Melody, a few friends, and my dreams that kept hope alive in those dark years of my life. I knew deep down that I was special and that I had a story to tell that would change the world.

When I attended college I had a new, enlightening and positive experience. Suddenly my environment was no longer a warzone but a place of acceptance, friendship, and empowerment. During my college years my gifts, talents and dreams were given wings. The experience of belonging healed the hurt of my past, and the dark clouds of doubt and fear began to dissipate. I could see a good future ahead of me.

After graduating from college I continued my education. I received a certification in Radio Broadcasting and a Master's Degree in Counseling. During this season of life I experienced

"The moment the crown was placed on my head a powerful emotion of joy and triumph came over me."

a lot of chaos. My college experience dwindled and I moved around a lot living in bachelorette pads, working part time just to stay afloat financially. There were times in this season that I felt like my dreams would never come true. I did not know what good things awaited me.

When I graduated with my Master's Degree I started my motivational speaking business and moved into my own apartment. Stability and hope were being rebuilt in this time. I started an anti-bullying campaign, "The Power of Words," which was inspired by my own experiences with words in my life. Over several years I gradually built my speaking business in my local community. I began to feel a strong desire to take my business and story out into the world beyond my community. In 2013 I competed for the title of Ms. Wheelchair Washington, a pageant for women who use wheelchairs for mobility. "The Power of Words" was my platform and I won the title! This opened the doors for my anti-bullying campaign statewide. Several months later I competed for the title Ms. Wheelchair America in the national pageant. In preparation for the pageant I was eager to win, knowing that winning the title would open national doors for my life and business. So I prepared earnestly and I won the title of Ms. Wheelchair America 2014! The moment the crown was placed on my head a powerful emotion of joy and triumph came over me.

Through my year as Ms. Wheelchair America I have spoken in schools, churches and businesses. I have sung and danced for national audiences. I have adaptive skied, adaptive surfed, met new and interesting people and packed enough adventure into one year to last a lifetime. Now that my reign is over, I foresee many more opportunities ahead to continue growing my business and changing the world. My dreams have come true!!

"Knowing your story, and being able to clearly articulate the message of your story, will open doors for you to change the world around you in a positive way."

CHAPTER 1 QUESTIONS

We all have a story. Your story is comprised of your unique personality, circumstances, personal choices and life experiences. Your story is powerful and carries a message to everyone you interact with in your daily life. Knowing your story, and being able to clearly articulate the message of your story, will open doors for you to change the world around you in a positive way.

What are a few key life experiences that shape your story?

_____

_____

_____

_____

_____

_____

_____

_____

What message does your story speak to the world?

_____

_____

_____

_____

_____

_____

_____

_____

What limitations have you over-come in your life?

What are your dreams for your life?

_____

_____

_____

_____

_____

_____

_____

_____

What are your short and long term goals?

_____

_____

_____

_____

_____

_____

_____

_____

ACTION STEP

This week, practice telling your story by sharing it with some-one you don't know.

CHAPTER 2:
YOUR WORDS HAVE POWER

"When good, true, encouraging words are spoken over someone, those words create a projected reality."

My story and life experience demonstrate the power of words. There have been many seasons in my life, both in my youth and my adulthood, in which the input of the words spoken by others around me was mostly negative. During those seasons I felt anxious, stressed, terrified, beaten down and worthless. In my travels I have spoken to many audiences and I always ask them to give me feedback as to how they felt when they were teased or bullied, or when they were the one that carried out the action of teasing or bullying. Across the board I have heard people of all ages describe the experience of negative words as hurtful, damaging, and diminishing. I have also experienced the power of positive words and the healing they bring to the experiences of hurt and negativity. My dreams have been cultivated through the encouraging words of mentors, teachers, friends, family and kind strangers. When words are said, they have metaphysical powers that affect the world. Words have power!

When good, true, encouraging words are spoken over someone, those words create a projected reality. Every day I realize amazing things that are happening in my life because of the encouraging words that have been spoken to me and over me. We have all been through times and will go through times in which we are surrounded with more negativity than positivity. This experience is not where any of us want to live. In our humanity we are inherently unable to thrive emotionally when surrounded by negativity. I have also experienced profound seasons of positivity. In these seasons I experienced healing, wholeness, and well-being. I have also asked audiences how they felt when they experienced positive words whether giving or receiving them. Every audience has said they felt built up, happy, and empowered. Obviously, this is what we all yearn to experience. We all thrive in positive environments.

One of the most profound experiences we can have is to have someone recognize who we are and say it out loud to us. The most healing experiences I have had in my life was when teachers, mentors, and peers empowered me to discover my design and identity as an individual by speaking words of life

"One of the most profound experiences we can have is to have someone recognize who we are and say it out loud to us."

to me. You have the ability to not only unlock your own gifts and talents, but also the gifts of those around you through your words and actions. I can attest that negative words have the power to block others from feeling valued. When individuals feel undervalued, they don't feel the freedom to take risks or be seen by others. A negative environment makes people hide in self-protection. Whereas, a positive environment creates a nurturing atmosphere where others' gifts and talents can be discovered and nurtured, allowing everyone to flourish. By making the choice to treat others well and speak kind and true words, you can change your school, family and the whole world for good.

Everyone experiences seasons in their life where they are surrounded by more negativity than positivity. These seasons can be dream squelchers. We can feel that our dreams are so far away because we are just merely surviving the battle. These seasons can leave us with a lot of destructive mindsets about ourselves and the world around us. There is a way to be free from the residue of these experiences. The first and most important thing you need to do to be free from the hurt of negativity is to forgive. Forgiveness is POWERFUL! When you forgive, you are not only freeing yourself from bitterness, but you are releasing the ones you forgive to be free from their offense. When you extend forgiveness to those who have hurt you, you are empowered to begin to speak life to those around you. The second is to recognize the negative words that you have mistakenly believed about yourself, confront them, and re-record them with uplifting truths about yourself and your life. The words you believe and speak to yourself have just as much power as the words that are spoken to you!

"Every day you have the choice as to whether you will create a negative or positive environment around you, simply by your words and actions."

CHAPTER 2 QUESTIONS

Every day you have the choice as to whether you will create a negative or positive environment around you, simply by your words and actions. Your words have power! Words leave a lasting impact on others. I hope that you will make a positive choice every single day to make the world around you a good place to be. My hope is that you will enter the next season of your life knowing who you are, and where you are going because you have been nurtured and have nurtured your peers around you with encouragement.

What negative words do you need to re-record with positive ones?

_____

_____

_____

_____

_____

_____

_____

_____

Who do you need to forgive?

What changes would you like to see in the world around you?

_____

_____

_____

_____

_____

_____

_____

_____

How can you be that change?

_____

_____

_____

_____

_____

_____

_____

_____

ACTION STEP

Every day this week, intention-
ally speak an encouraging word
to someone around you. Watch
what happens!

CHAPTER 3:
YOUR GIFTS AND TALENTS

"Gifts and talents are invisible riches."

My unique abilities are singing, dancing, public speaking, writing and oil painting, to name a few. I write my own songs and motivational presentations, choreograph dances in my wheelchair, write books and create beautiful art, all with partial limbs. Partial limbs are my one disability, but I have many abilities! I discovered my strengths, gifts and talents over time through the encouragement of peers, mentors and family, who recognized my talents through observation and then told me through positive feedback what they saw. I also recognized them because they came naturally. When I sing I feel alive. You can't stop me from moving and dancing. I stole the microphone away from the announcer at a rodeo when I was four years old. As I have grown and matured so have my strengths, gifts and talents. The journey that I have taken to get to where I am today was not easy, but through faith, choosing good friends and investing time and effort into my direction in life, I have been set on a path of discovery, to discover my gifts, talents, and purpose in life.

Traveling with my motivational speaking business, I have observed that as I share my gifts and talents in the world it changes people's lives; it gives people hope that they can pursue their dreams and purpose, too. Seek and you will find. Just as I have discovered my gifts, you will too. I have the daily challenge of living my life with partial limbs, but my gifts and talents give me the tools to live victoriously. I have one disability, yet I have many abilities. And these talents, when I let them shine, do more in the world than arms and legs ever could.

Gifts and talents are invisible riches. Your gifts and talents lie within your being. They are not tangible and cannot be seen with the eye, but they are real and when you allow your invisible riches to shine in the world, they draw true value into your life and the lives of others.

"You will feel alive when you are functioning in your talents."

Every individual is born with strengths, gifts, and talents. You may be artistic, or geared towards the sciences. You may be athletic or great with people. You may be a thinker or inventor. Your unique abilities come naturally. You will feel alive when you are functioning in your talents. The wonderful thing about your talents is that they help you overcome challenges in life, and when taken into the world, also create positive change.

Learn your strengths, gifts and talents by studying yourself. The most effective way to grow in your gifts and talents is to surround yourself with peers and mentors who will invest in your personal development, positive people who will speak encouraging words into your life. It is also important for you to speak positive words to others, for you will attract what you put out into the world.

"When you know who you are, you become unstoppable!"

CHAPTER 3 QUESTIONS

When you know who you are, you become unstoppable! Under-standing your personal identity will make you more resilient against the negativity that life can throw at you. You are young and have so much ahead of you. Be a student of yourself and your peers around you. Learn your gifts and talents. Discover the things that make you feel alive! Then let your unique abili-ties shine and watch them change the world!

What makes you feel alive?

_____

_____

_____

_____

_____

_____

_____

_____

What abilities come naturally to you?

What would you like to learn about yourself?

_____

_____

_____

_____

_____

_____

_____

_____

What abilities do you see in others around you?

_____

_____

_____

_____

_____

_____

_____

_____

ACTION STEP

Ask someone close to you, who you know wishes the best for you, what gifts and talents they see in you.

CHAPTER 4:
YOU HAVE A DREAM

"Discover your dreams, follow them and help others do the same."

From early childhood I was a dreamer. I dreamed of being a famous singer, public speaker, performer and traveling the world. As an adult I can say, my dreams are coming true. I have become all of those things, and there are still dreams that have yet to come true. The fruition of these dreams took discipline and determination on my part. There were times I felt lost and unsure if my dreams would ever come true. There are dreams in my life still to be fulfilled. My future dreams are, to be a talk show host, get married and have a family and be an International Evangelist. I have learned, while living a few years on this earth, that dreams mature as we mature. There is no greater joy in life than a dream fulfilled.

Many of us believe that dreams are fulfilled when a magical genie, or fairy godmother shows up and grants our every wish, or we when are lucky enough to win the lottery. A true dream is not make believe. You must prepare for your dreams by aligning your gifts with action in order for them to be fulfilled. You must also make space to receive the fulfillment of your dreams into your life. And, dreams also require faith. Much of preparing for a dream is believing in something and its ability to happen that has not yet happened. As you begin your journey toward your dreams, look ahead and prepare today for what you believe will happen in your future.

Our dreams start to matriculate at an early age. Our strengths, personality traits, and interests are solidified in us by the time we are four years old. Your dream is a part of you, it is tied to your identity and as you grow and mature your dreams will be realized. The obstacles that block our dreams are often not circumstantial but instead a lack of growth and progress within ourselves. Issues like addiction, abuse, unhealthy friendships, and misaligned life choices can stunt our maturity and our dreams. The best choice you can make to fulfill the dreams you have for your life is to make life decisions aligned with your dreams. Where ever a misaligned choice is made, life progress stops, dream progression stops. Yet where ever an aligned choice is made, life progress begins. Discover your dreams, follow them and help others do the same. Go and be a dream builder!

"A dream fulfilled is the reward awaiting us in the horizon of our life."

CHAPTER 4 QUESTIONS

A dream is something good you want to see happen in your life and in the world. The amazing thing is that when you fulfill your dreams, it not only benefits you, but it also brings goodness into the world and changes people's lives in a positive way. You have a dream! Dream beyond limitations! Look into the future and project the best outcome of your life. Your dreams are like arrows pointing and leading you towards your destiny. Dreams keep us motivated to persevere through the trials and tribulations of life. A dream fulfilled is the reward awaiting us in the horizon of our life.

If money were no issue, what would be your dream come true?

_____

_____

_____

_____

_____

_____

_____

_____

How does your dream benefit you and others?

What are some practical steps you need to take to achieve your dreams?

_____

_____

_____

_____

_____

_____

_____

_____

Are there any misaligned choices you are making to stunt your growth?

What are some changes you would like to make to grow your dreams?

_____

_____

_____

_____

_____

_____

_____

_____

ACTION STEP

Share your dream out loud with someone you trust to invest in your life. There is so much power in sharing your dream; it creates energy to make it a reality.

CHAPTER 5:
YOU CAN START A REVOLUTION

"When you become an individual without walls, with limitless creative liberties, you become a force of good in the world."

We are all born into a world that has more walls than wide open space, more rules than creative opportunities and more hardship than freedom. But you do not have to accept these challenges as your reality for the rest of your life. It is important to know what you're up against so you can be savvy and capable of navigating life's challenges.

I believe as a human being you are inherently designed to be in touch with nature and free to live life with wide open space for adventure, creativity, and relationships. The world around us does not intrinsically provide these opportunities; you must search for these experiences yourself. In order to break free from the walls of life and find that place of freedom, you must know who you are. You are powerful, more powerful than you know! You are capable of breaking down the walls of life and the tools needed to break down the walls are held within your identity and your gifts. Being the pure, honest YOU requires that you take the road less traveled, that you face your fears and take risks, and take many leaps of faith. The journey toward wide open space in your existence can be lonely and difficult. You must decide that the opinion of others is less important than your freedom. When you arrive in the wide open space, every challenge you faced to get there is so worth it. The challenges and obstacles that you will overcome to break down the walls of life will only make you wiser, stronger and kinder for the journey.

When you become an individual without walls, with limitless creative liberties, you become a force of good in the world. I believe that the rat race of life keeps us occupied, but not truly productive. Being productive is living your life not only to have your needs met but to do good in the world and meet the needs of others. There is so much good that needs to be done in the world, starving children that need to be fed, hurting hearts that need to be healed and poverty that needs to be provided with resources. When you are free you can answer to these needs and receive the reward that comes from living a purposeful life. Your gifts and talents, your story and dreams are the answer. Your true identity will start a revolution!

"The secret to becoming a revolutionary person is to acknowledge that nagging sense that something needs to change in the world around you."

CHAPTER 5 QUESTIONS

Everyone has the capability of being revolutionary. The secret to becoming a revolutionary person is to acknowledge that nagging sense that something needs to change in the world around you. It is easy to become numb in the rigmarole of everyday life. Look beyond the minutiae of everyday and open your eyes to injustice, beauty, pain, and good. Be the one to fight and believe for progress in the world.

What walls of life do you perceive around you right now?

_____

_____

_____

_____

_____

_____

_____

_____

What is your plan to break past these walls?

_____

_____

_____

_____

_____

_____

_____

_____

What good do you want to do in the world?

_____

_____

_____

_____

_____

_____

_____

_____

What legacy do you want to leave in the world?

_____

_____

_____

_____

_____

_____

_____

_____

ACTION STEP

On a white board, piece of paper or computer, write down the revolution you believe you are meant to start. Then write three steps you need to take to accomplish the change you want to see in the world. Hang this where you can see it every day.

CHAPTER 6:
YOU HAVE A CHOICE

"When you make a decision to accept love into your life, you become someone who can give love and bring good to the world around you."

When I graduated from high school my self-esteem was very low. I experienced positive encouragement in my college years, which changed my life in a positive way. My heartfelt wish for you is that you enter the next season of your life with a strong sense of self and a strong sense of direction because you know your identity and your destiny.

My destiny is being fulfilled because people made the choice around me to speak encouragement to me, though ultimately it was my choice to receive into my heart what they said, set short term and long term goals, go to school, get my Master's Degree, be patient through the hard times and keep going until I saw my dreams coming true!! There was a long period of time where I felt invisible and powerless. During that time I was discouraged and I had my doubts as to whether I would ever be living my dreams. I distinctly remember making a choice in my mind that I would keep trying, praying, hoping and walking in the direction of my destiny until I saw it come into fruition. I had divine help! My faith in God and my Christian walk has been the one source of help, hope and strength.

When we experience healing through an encounter with love, we can then bring healing to others. You have a choice everyday as to how you will live your life. When you make a decision to accept love into your life, you become someone who can give love and bring good to the world around you.

The direction of your life is a choice. You have gifts and talents, you have passions and dreams, and in order for them to come into fruition, you must make the decision to take the practical steps towards achieving them. Dreams don't just drop into your life. As someone said, dreams don't come true, we must become true to them! It takes discipline and fortitude to follow and fulfill your dreams, and it is so worth it!

"The change in your school and the world around you starts with you."

CHAPTER 6 QUESTIONS

You have a choice as to whether you will bring good or harm to the world around you. The change in your school and the world around you starts with you. You are the one who can speak encouraging words to those around you. You are the one who can create a positive environment that builds the gifts, talents, identities and destinies of others. You are the one who can start a revolution.

Will you be the one to build your dreams and those of others?

_____

_____

_____

_____

_____

_____

_____

_____

What revolution do you believe you are meant to start?

_____

_____

_____

_____

_____

_____

_____

_____

What changes do you wish to see in the world?

_____

_____

_____

_____

_____

_____

_____

_____

What action steps do you need to take to start a revolution?

_____

_____

_____

_____

_____

_____

_____

_____

ACTION STEP

Take one big leap of faith this week that you have been holding off out of fear or doubt.

www.ingramcontent.com/pod-product-compliance
Lightning Source LLC
Chambersburg PA
CBHW041531090426
42738CB00036B/115